7 Secrets of Successful Influencer Marketing Campaigns

Internet Primer Series

By Matt Frary

SmarterChaos.com Inc.
340 3rd Street
Castle Rock, CO 80104

www.smarterchaos.com

DISCLAIMER

This booklet has been written to provide information about developing a successful podcast that will impress all who hear it. Every effort has been taken to make this booklet as complete, helpful and accurate as possible.

This booklet is intended to be educational and instructional. The author and/or the publisher do not guarantee that the information contained in this booklet is comprehensive or complete, and will not be responsible for any errors or omissions. The author and/or publisher bear neither liability nor responsibility to any person or entity with respect to any loss or damage caused or alleged to be caused directly or indirectly by the information in this booklet.

TABLE OF CONTENTS

ABOUT MATT FRARY

Matt Frary has been involved in online marketing and customer lead generation for over 15 years and is the founder and CEO of SmarterChaos, where he has realized his true potential as the "Chief of Chaos". SmarterChaos is a performance marketing agency that helps advertisers find the right user at the right time on the right media partner's website.

Matt learned the power of affiliate marketing early in his career when he got a job placing advertisements on travel websites for a luggage company. He then moved on to work with a charity mall, managing relationships with companies such as Amazon, eBay and Barnes and Noble.

He has also worked for Microsoft building lead generation channels for automobiles, and did an internship with Mercedes Benz where he created a marketing plan for the launch of their "smart car" in the U.S.

He has managed affiliate networks that turn over tens of millions of dollars per year in revenue, with over 1,600 advertisers and 60,000 affiliates involved.

He has a Bachelor's Degree in marketing and business from the University of Colorado, with concentrations in Russian, finance and brand marketing. He also has an MBA from Thunderbird Graduate School.

Matt is sought after speaker on pay for performance marketing, lead generation and ethical marketing practices. He is also the host of the podcast **Chaos Makes Sense.**

INTRODUCTION

HOW TO UNLOCK THE POWER OF INFLUENCER MARKETING IN YOUR BUSINESS AND A PEEK INTO THE *POKÉMON GO* PHENOMENON

Hi, I'm Matt Frary, and I'm excited to tell you that one of the most effective ways to get your product in front of potential buyers these days, is to unleash the power of influencer marketing. Influencers are the "mover and shakers" in their chosen fields and have built strong followings that you can tap into, if you know how to develop working relationships with them.

Influencers can be found in every industry. Take horse racing for example.

I was recently down in Kentucky (I travel a lot for business and that's the beauty of the affiliate marketing and influencer lifestyle, we can travel all the time, we can work on the road, and work on our business while we're doing lots of fun and exciting things) and while I went to a stud farm where racehorse **American Pharaoh** studs up to three times a day. Talk about an influencer for that sport! This horse is a Triple Crown winner and worth *$200 million!* Naturally I jumped in, grabbed his neck and took a selfie.

I can tell you, it was very exciting!

And then you have the **Pokémon GO phenomenon** that's sweeping the globe at the moment. It's another prime example of influencer marketing at work and I can't believe it! To watch these Pokémon gyms springing up at the White House, and at the Pentagon . . . I'm wondering where it's all going. I don't think it's going to get anybody paying any more attention to each other, but hopefully it does get them outside and engaged.

And I think that's really the key. I'm looking forward in the future to dissecting this case study, of how Pokémon GO became a phenomenon so quickly – it *already* has more users than Twitter!

It's absolutely insane but there has to be a way *your* business can tap into this, right? There sure is, and my business partner, Beth Lazar, and I know the secrets to launching a successful influencer marketing campaign.

Here's why.

Together we have built the Pollen-8 Influencer Network, where we have been working with businesses to create powerful influencer campaigns for them. Beth is the CEO of the Pollen-8 Influencer Network and CTO/ Chief of Strategy at SmarterChaos, and has an MS in Information Systems. She has a passion for technology and how it can improve a business.

We saw a *huge* opportunity within the Pollen-8 platform to simplify and streamline the influencer process. Our system focuses on increasing revenue for advertisers, and assisting influencers to create interesting content that drives traffic to their own websites and social media platforms.

And it's through this experience that we've come up with the **7 Secrets of Successful Influencer Marketing Campaigns**, and what's more, we are going to share these with you right here in this booklet . . . for free!

So please, read through them and then use them in your business.

When companies like Reuters report that currently around **47% of online users are using ad-blocking technology**, it's vital that your business finds new ways to reach potential customers. That's why those in the know are turning to content produced by influencers, and their ability to convince people to buy the products they recommend, just by interacting with them on the internet and social media.

This **7 Secrets of Successful Influencer Marketing Campaigns** booklet will help you get a slice of the action, and if you have questions or require assistance with your online performance marketing, you can reach me and my team at SmarterChaos.com, or on Facebook at facebook.com/smarterchaos.

Ok, let's get started.

SECRET #1
INFLUENCERS ARE NOT FREE

The first secret advertisers need to understand is that influencers **are not free** – especially with the *massive* growth that has occurred recently in the influencer arena.

There are only a limited number of influencers that have high traffic, and most of them are not willing to work on performance at this point. You may get the occasional one who is, and there are some who will work on a hybrid-type arrangement, but you're still looking at (on the low side) paying these guys between $150-$500 per sponsored post or video.

However, I would say the standard amount is probably between $1,000 and $3,000, but I've seen this go as high as **$14,000 dollars** for a sponsored post! This was paid to a *big* YouTuber who had about 1.5 million subscribers.

It's something I see a lot. An advertiser who has a large brand or a super-interesting product (and maybe they feel like they have found the gold on the internet with what they're offering) will come to me to talk about building an influencer program and, a lot of times, they expect influencers to run campaigns for free. Or in exchange for just a product.

Those days are gone.

What they need to realize is, there are so many people reaching out to the same pool of influencers – people with big names like GQ and others – that it's difficult for the influencers to see through the noise without some sort of budget being presented for a sponsorship. It puts the influencer in a really interesting place, because the influencer *gains* a lot of power.

I'll give you an example.

Take the well-known company **Nestle**. They have 25 major brands and a huge digital strategy marketing team. Even a company as large as Nestle is looking at influencers and how influencers can drive their brands! So you can bet that influencers have figured out that if Nestle is chasing them, and you have widget x, y, z, that you want promoted, that you're going to have to probably pay some money to get them to talk about your product.

If you want access to their audience, you're going to have to pay their rates and whatever it is that they're asking for, but hopefully with huge results.

This can be scary for smaller advertisers because they don't necessarily see how they're going to recoup this level of investment. But, if you're going to have a successful influencer program, it's just something you're going to have to budget for.

Now, there are some **non-financial** compensations that you can provide to influencers – like shout outs on your social media to help them drive traffic to their site – but for the most part, you're looking at sponsored posts and sponsored videos at this point in time.

So there you have it – influencers are NOT free, and building an influencer program is going to take a little (if not quite a bit) of cash, and you're going to need to make an investment in that.

SECRET #2
BE PREPARED TO INVEST TIME

The number two secret is that you need to be prepared to invest some time in your influencer program.

What? You mean bloggers just don't pick up the phone? Instagrammers aren't just jumping out at you trying to run your products? What...?

Yeah, it's amazing.

But again, they're being bombarded so much, and even if you're using an opted-in influencer network like Pollen-8 (where anybody in the network has opted-in to receive these kind of offers) you're going to have to expect to spend quite a bit of time managing the influencers through the entire workflow.

There's more to it than just contacting them. Honestly it's taking me or my team, on average, about 5-7 requests before we even get responses from a lot of the influencers that haven't opted-in already. So, there's quite a bit of back and forth in terms of trying to get these guys to respond, and even at that point you're only getting about a **20% response rate**.

So you need to build a list of influencers and go after this target market of people you think would fit your brand, and then reach out to them, which does take some time.

So your plan is this:

1. Build the list (you've got to figure out who to target). And then...
2. Find their contact info

How to go about finding their contact info

Once again, there are various methods of doing this. There are the opted-in networks that, hopefully, these target influencers are a part of. But if they're not, you're essentially using other tools that may be able to spider the web or grab that information for you. Otherwise you are literally going to have to visit each website and dig around looking for contact information . . . or go through their social media accounts . . .

This is extremely time consuming.

So, unless you're like me and have a super cool partner like Beth Lazar who can build the right tools for you (because she's always at home coding instead of doing things like going to see American Pharaoh!), you are going to have to spend *a massive amount of time doing this manually.*

You will have to spend weekends and every spare hour going after these influencers – and some of them even have *agents* you have to go through. It's true! And I don't just mean the bigger guys; I'm talking mid-tier folks who don't have huge followings.

The PR companies have swooped in and picked up these influencers and inserted themselves as agents, just to help drive their rates up and take a piece of it for themselves.

Make no mistake – there's the whole act of not only contacting these influencers, but negotiating them either with them or their PR firm. I was at a wedding recently in Detroit and I actually met someone that told me their job description is an "influencer agent."

Of course, there have always been talent agents around in other industries. These agents are really the gate keeper between the production and producers, and the talent. They keep all things fair for all parties. But are far as influencers using agents . . . it's really new. I'm curious to see what the future holds.

It's fun watching these new markets spring up, but at the end of the day it's going to take a lot of time to learn about this market, learn how to access the influencers, and to find out what they're responding to.

To show just how far this can go, I even heard one story from YouTube's studios out there in Los Angeles, that YouTubers are buying billboards now, and actually soliciting via billboards to be on their channel and, basically, to pay them to recommend products.

It's a whole new culture, so be prepared to invest time!

Now for the next secret.

SECRET #3
PROVIDE FREE STUFF

The next secret to successful influencer marketing is to be prepared to provide free stuff. At the bare *minimum* you want to be able to provide your influencers with review products.

You know, the whole idea behind influencer marketing is to provide authentic reviews, and that's not really possible if the person who is reviewing these products has never had the chance to touch them, test them, wear them (whatever the products are), and then photograph or video them. Being able to do this is really important in terms of the content that they're providing.

Two years ago, when influencer marketing was really coming about, all you had to provide was a coupon code. You could say: "Hey, you've got $20 off of this product, Mrs. Influencer. Try it out, let us know and please make a blog post."

That was literally all you had to do - provide a coupon.

But it's not the case any longer.

I use to say things to bloggers like: "Don't you want to be associated with this awesome brand? Go buy the product and talk about it."

So it has changed in two years, and you need to be willing to provide free stuff and, sometimes, you need to be doing this every month – especially if you find an influencer who has driven quite a few sales for you. That might mean sending them free giveaway products to encourage social sharing on a regular basis.

All these all types of things are really important to keep an ongoing relationship with the influencer, or else you risk having your content move down the pipeline and nobody seeing it anymore.

You have got to keep them engaged.

Give everybody a visual. I have worked with this YouTuber called ShadesOfKassie, and we would send her a product – let's say makeup for example. She would go on YouTube and do 20 minutes of unboxing this product.

She would talk about the shades of lipstick, and the type of eyeshadow, and how it made her feel. Granted, she was beautiful and influential and everybody wanted to watch her channel, but we could see spikes in sales of *$10,000 in a day* from her unboxing a product we had sent to her!

She's a great influencer, and it shows that you need to provide your product to them and let them have that experience. Think about it. Does your family buy much without experiencing it, and aren't the purchase decisions usually made by someone influencing your family to make that purchase?

Absolutely, right?

And it can be a recommendation from a family member, or a friend, or something along those lines, or a review on a website such as Amazon. com. Potential buyers go to a site like Amazon, see the reviews and see what people are saying about the products. Or it can be YouTube reviews or YouTube unboxings. I love going on YouTube and researching the different options when I'm looking at different products to buy, and watching the different reviews and unboxings and really getting some relevant information from that.

Have you heard about the kid who has made over a million dollars by unboxing all the toys that he's sent, and he does it on YouTube?

It just goes to show, you have to send out products and get in these influencer's lives. You have to become so ingrained, and part of what they're doing, that they'll talk about you.

Alright, so now you know that influencers are not free, and that you have to be prepared to invest time and provide free stuff. Let's move on to the next secret.

SECRET #4
KNOW YOUR REAL AUDIENCE

You *must* know who your *real* audience is, and not just *assume* you know who they are.

I have worked with clients before that were pretty adamant their demographic had certain characteristics, but in reality the correct influencers for them were the ones that had common interests and common market segments. And you have got to get your head around the fact that there is also potential in abstract variables, such as attitudes and self-image, and maybe even expertise in a particular field, and you need to be looking at all of that.

I've found with some advertisers that they'll come to you with a profile of who they think their product reaches, but I would say that a lot of times that's off – *they don't actually know their audience!*

And sometimes you get an advertiser who knows their audience, but you have to tweak and tune what you're offering to influencers through looking at it from their perspective and specific requirements.

You need to look for that person with the right attitude, or the person that has that expertise.

If you look at an online business like Dollar Shave Club, which was a client of ours at smarterchaos.com, they really believed that their influencers were the sport sites, the manly man sites, and things like that.

But I think that over time, they realized that it's probably the girlfriend, or the wife, that's buying the razors and spending money on those types of things. So you need to really take a look at not only who the end user is, but also who's *influencing* the purchase decision.

And it's not all about the numbers either; you're not just looking for somebody who has high YouTube subscribers, because you know YouTube stars are going to be influential for the younger crowd, but might not be influential for some older, mommy product.

It's not all about the numbers.

Just because the numbers are high doesn't necessarily make it a good fit. You have to understand and work with the influencer, and make sure that they are the right person for the particular product that you're trying to promote.

So knowing the audience of the influencer - and sometimes even the influencer doesn't totally know their audience – is difficult and that's why it is good to go with a network like **Pollen-8**. We've worked with a whole range of influencers before, and we have tools to find out their reach. That's why one of the biggest reasons to work with someone like **Pollen-8** is we can help figure out what kind of audience you should actually be going after.

SECRET #5
IT'S ABOUT THE BRAND,
NOT THE SALES

What you need to understand as an advertiser when you're launching a campaign is that obviously the intention is to increase your overall sales and conversions. But you have to understand that you're also driving additional customer engagement through these social media conversations, and people are talking about pretty much everything, including what products to use.

That's a huge influence in terms of people wanting to check out your product, and learn more about your product, with the intention of buying it.

And these social influencers are also creating valuable content for the advertisers, like testimonials and quotes, and maybe even some non-traditional content that can be a valuable marketing asset for the brand itself. And with a lot of this type of content, it's not targeted or created – *it just happens organically.*

In the age of digital marketing, everything seems measurable.

There are tools and strategies available, and everybody is out there talking about measuring attribution and how to attribute incremental sales to the marketing efforts that you're doing.

We live this every single day at Smarter Chaos, where we moonlight as advertising agents. With our largest brands, they want to measure everything; they want to measure *exactly* how many sales, in a very binary way, e.g. I made this placement, I put this on this website, and I got this many sales. But it doesn't always work that way.

Obviously everybody wants to track results, and there are definitely methods for tracking your influencer's click through rate and all those terms that everybody likes to attribute to digital marketing. There are methods for doing that, but there's also the value that you get from the *additional* content being generated through the conversations that are taking place about your brand.

Take it from Trump.

You at least need somebody talking about you, no matter how they're talking about you! Tongue-in-cheek aside, it's all about somebody talking about you, and people having a conversation about your brand. And you may not be able to completely control these channels in terms of what people are saying, but you also can't completely measure what's going on with the brand.

That's the beauty of it – it can spread like wildfire like Pokémon GO, or a lot of other brands like Dollar Shave Club, and be a very successful way to get your product out there. That's the "X Factor" at work, and it's something that can't be measured.

SECRET #6
INFLUENCER MARKETING
DOES NOT STAND ALONE

Everyone needs to understand that influencer marketing is *one* component of their overall digital strategy. It needs to be part of a larger, widespread marketing program that looks at all of the other traditional methods of digital marketing.

This includes search, social, affiliate . . . everything. This is just one component of it, and if you're not investing in your brand, influencers aren't going to invest time promoting your brand. You need to continue to invest in those marketing channels with the best return, and then engage influencers to add credibility to your brand and get people talking about it.

Not long ago I went to LA and I did a tour of all these high fashion companies and super sexy internet companies, and all of them said, "Oh, we don't need any other kind of marketing because we have influencers and they are influencing our brand."

Then I would ask them the question, "That's great, how's that going for you?"

And they'd say, "Well it's going really good – except there's just a couple issues. One is our sales are declining, and two it's cyclical, so we only get sales when they talk about us."

So, okay, glad that's working for you! You're all set!

All kidding aside, that is literally some of the things that I've heard. Of course, what they should have said is, "We've got this great influencer program and now we need to do something else, and so we're exploring that with them."

There is a net positive effect that happens when you add search, and paid social, and re-targeting, and affiliate marketing, and all of these different things together – and they all have to be in conjunction with your influencer program, and tied together.

This applies to every promotion you're doing, every communication, all your brand messaging, and it all has to be integrated with your influencer program, and be one common thing.

Right, and getting to the last tip – I don't want to be a spoiler, but I guess I'm going to just lob this like a softball . . . is everybody else doing this?

SECRET #7
BECAUSE IT WORKS

Everybody's doing it. And the reason why everybody's doing it is, it works.

We see stats like 92% of buyers trust recommendations from individuals versus brands directly, and that's the reason why advertisers are jumping all over the influencer band wagon. Most advertisers that have done it, and have implemented an effective strategy for influencers, have judged it to be effective. They feel they have actually acquired better customers with a longer lifetime value, which is interesting.

Take my wife for example.

When she's talking with her girlfriends or friends and one of them has purchased a new kitchen widget, or something cool for their kids, you can guarantee that within the week it will be in my household . . . and I've purchased it, whether I wanted to or not!

I'll be darned if Hollie up the street said it was the best thing, and the kids loved it, and we're better parents for buying it, and they're safer – you better believe we're buying it.

We all have things that we have to have and people that we follow in the footsteps of. So I think that's the very idea of influencer marketing; somebody recommends something that we just cannot live without. And I'll tell you, if that *one brand* is getting in your household, the *rest of the brands* should be trying to get in your household. It's becoming a world of influence out there.

It's all about getting in the hearts and the minds of these influencers and, if you follow all the different secrets and tips you've been given here, you're going to realize it takes time, and it takes money, and it takes commitment, and you have to integrate it with the rest of your marketing. You've also got to give them some free stuff, and focus on the branding, and know who your audiences are.

Realize you're not alone.

Everybody else is doing it, and you're going to need to do it better than they are.

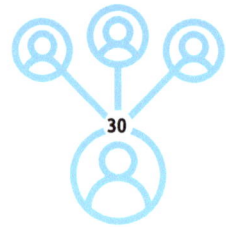

CONCLUSION

SO THERE YOU HAVE IT – THE 7 SECRETS OF SUCCESSFUL INFLUENCER MARKETING CAMPAIGNS

Now that I've spilled the beans, I guess they aren't secrets anymore! That's ok, I know everyone who reads this booklet will find this information is extremely valuable when it comes to promoting their business.

And if you need further advice or information on your influencer campaigns, please feel free to contact Beth or myself, and we will be more than happy to help.

340 3rd St
Castle Rock, CO 80104

Telephone: (720) 583-1136
Website: www.smarterchaos.com

 Twitter.com/@smarterchaos
Facebook.com/smarterchaos

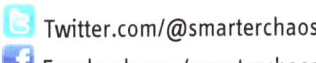

#121 - 200 S. Wilcox St.
Castle Rock, CO 80104 US

Telephone: (888) 989-0069

Email: contactus@pollen-8.com
Website: www.pollen-8.com